Living With The Enemy

by Paula Julson

LIVING WITH THE ENEMY

First edition. January 13, 2025.

ISBN: 979-8230869306

Written by Paula Julson.

Table of Contents

Preface

MAN-HATER. We, as women, have all been called this a time, or two in our lives. It is a term that describes a woman with boundaries and demands more for herself than what she receives. The more respect she requires, the more she is committed to fending off the opposite sex.

Why is it that women are accused of overreacting when they refuse to laugh at a sexist joke, or a thoughtless remark? Why are we labeled "frigid", just because we can't forget all the sins committed against us, during the day, fast enough, for you to enjoy our bodies at bedtime? Let me get this straight...we are to act as mindless idiots, with no feelings, or standards, just so you can have your pleasure when needed? You are not required to put forth any effort during the day, to ensure affection in the evening? Is your sex life that stagnant and motionless, where you are in no need of any current, or flow?

Women are not cattle. We are not bred for your needs only. We are not to be used up and deemed useless when the gray hairs start showing up and we stop flowing every month. Here, I'll put it in the most simple way I can for you. You are not getting laid because you are lazy and ignorant.

Women have needs, just like you. Why do men feel we can go for days without constructive conversation, any show of affection, or appreciation, and still stir desire within us at the snap of a finger? You purposely starve our fires of passion of any oxygen, then complain about the smoldering embers, as they die. You were in charge of tending to that fire. You let the flames go out. You didn't do your job. Quit laying the blame on us.

You require attention. You require recognition. You require answers to your questions. You wish for us to respect you and your needs. Then, why should women not require the same? Who told you that we are less? Who told you that we won't remember anything you say to us, and are numb to any pain?

Teach yourself some manners and get educated. Until then, I will remain a "manhater". I will not stoop to your level of disrespect, while expecting respect in return. I will not look the other way, with my eyes, ears, and lips closed. I was given a voice, an opinion, and you, dear sir, are going to hear it.

Introduction

Happy New Year! I'd like to believe that this year's lessons in love, and life, will teach me to be a better person. I am willing to look past all the lies and make-believe crap that I've been told, and act like I can move on from it, while still being a friend. But honestly, I don't think I can.

I feel as if I will continue to carry the hurt and fury in my heart throughout the whole year. Why am I always meant to struggle? Why is the person causing the pain living their best life, and able to sleep at night?

Am I to carry on and smile, like it didn't catch me behind the knees and knock me to the floor? To forgive and forget?

I will never forget how my "friend" and lover played me, then hurled me out of their life because I couldn't be what they expected in their wicked mind. How can I forget? Does healing require me to forget?

I went through this same scenario so many times with the same person, that they definitely won in the "how many times can I make her miserable" game. I have become so jaded and closed off. How am I to find love again?

I heard it said that there are people in this world that are just born to suffer. I believe I may be one of them. So many years trying to better my life, and why? When I am surely meant to suffer. Do I just give up and let anyone walk all over me? Do I suffer in silence, or am I meant to share my suffering with others?

The New Year is full of promise for most. But for me, I see repeated patterns and grief. I need to do something unexpected and drastic. I need an entirely new outlook. A new job. A new destination. Something to plan and look forward to. I declare that this year, I will take all the chances I can, in my continued quest for answers, and I will take you with me on my journey.

I believe I am to suffer aloud, and let my experiences help those in their suffering. My resolution is to not allow someone in their struggle, feel as if they are alone in this world. This book is to help anyone suffering the consequences of falling in love with a narcissist. It was a grave mistake but can be survived. I hope my book will give you the knowledge and courage to believe in yourself, once again, so that you are able to seek out the life that you desire. My wish is that you gain the courage to love yourself, as no other can.

CHAPTER ONE

Why Would I Live With A Narcissist?

There are many phenomena in this world that cannot be explained. The moon's relationship with the ocean tide, rainbows, the aurora borealis, the power of lightning...the list goes on, and on. But the one that may remain the biggest mystery of all, is how a strong and capable woman could even consider staying in a relationship with a narcissist. Mind boggling! But what we haven't considered, is that seventy-five percent of the human population these days could be considered a narcissist, by definition. We live in a society that has become self-serving and without empathy for others' feelings. When I began my healing journey, four years ago, I didn't even know what a narcissist was. Now, they are everywhere! It opened my eyes to what I was blind to all of my life, up until now of course. I came to realize that my own mother was the epitome of the word, and that the reason for a lot of my trauma response today, was from being raised in a narcissistic environment. I find that many are living in a world of "it's not my fault I am the way I am" society. As adults, we need to ask ourselves, if it's not your fault, then who's fault is it? How long can you go on blaming someone else for your current situation? Is that your response for everything today? Are you never going to take accountability for your life? Or are you just waiting for someone else to take the blame and spend the rest of **their** life trying to make up for **your** mistakes? Guess what? That is not only toxic, but sick.

So, the question is, why would a woman want to stay in a relationship with a narcissist?

I have found that one of the reasons, using my own personal experience, is that sometimes you can't just walk out and leave a not-so-nice situation at will. Especially if you are married or living with them. I'd like to say, and have on several occasions, that you need to get out and away from the narcissist as quickly as possible, any way you can. But I also know that those words of advice are not always the reality for everyone involved. Everyone has a different scenario going on in their life and sometimes they decide that where they are is tolerable, for now, because they need to buy some time for themselves, until they can plan their escape.

This book is not for the weak of heart. Choosing to tolerate a narcissist longer than you might like to, is not an easy task. You need to be of strong mind and will. It will also require healthy friendships. You will need an immense sense of self-worth and self-respect. You will learn to see past the narc's bullshit, to the point that you won't even flinch, when they come at you with their gaslighting tactics. But in order to get to this point, you need to do your research. You need to find out what makes them tick. You need to find the crack in their facade.

The one thing they all have in common, is that the narcissist enjoys studying people. You'll often see them by themselves amongst a group of people. They don't like to run in packs. They fly solo most of the time. Even in a group situation, you will find them preoccupied with something else. They will spend most of their available time watching, listening and comparing people. At first, they will give you their undying and somewhat creepy attention, on everything you have to say. They will watch intently, to all of your reactions to certain things. They will memorize the look on your face as you tell them about lost loves, or bad romances. They will remember things that you won't even remember disclosing to them. They want to be near you at all times, so as to "get to know you better". And you will get comfortable with their availability.

Then comes the love bombing. The gifts, along with exaggerated praise, and honor. All the flowers, weekend getaways, compliments, and all the romance you have ever dreamed about. They will seem to walk right out of your fantasies and then act as if they are the only ones that are able to give you the things that you crave. They convince you that no one else will ever love you the way they do. And get ready for action. Because instead of the relationship taking its time, it will seem to come at you all at once. They don't want to wait, because they know exactly what they want and won't hesitate to say "I love you", or start talking about future plans, even if it has only been a couple weeks. It will leave your head spinning and you feeling quite overwhelmed at times. But, once they have your undying attention and trust, is the moment the games begin. Remember this, if it seems too good to be true, it probably is.

They give and they take away. Just when you are getting used to their extreme generosity and aggressive affection, they will ghost you out of the blue, and conversation will become minimal. Here comes the separation anxiety that they are counting on. This is done to make you think that you have done something wrong or have offended them in some way. You haven't. But you will start second guessing yourself on something you might have said, or did, to cause this extremely odd behavior. They will go for days without a text, or a call. Your attempts will go directly to their voicemail. But don't worry. You haven't done anything wrong. This is a game they like to call "let's see how much they love me". And they will play it over and over again throughout your relationship. They never get tired of this mind game. They use this tactic to make you beg for their once upon a time, so easily given, love and attention that you grew to depend on. This is how they gain control of the relationship. By using your emotions. The ones that they have been studying, so intently, while you were inseparable. They will make you jump through invisible hoops you didn't know existed, just to talk to, or be close to them. And if they aren't being what you once thought, or expected them to be, well...it must be something that changed on your end, because they were "perfect" for you in the beginning. You must be the one who feels differently about them. See what I'm saying? Mind games. They turn it all back on you. The number one weapon of choice for the narcissist, and they couldn't exist without it. You will either fall prey to their words and actions, while spending the rest of your days wondering why they don't treat you right? Or, you can learn to deflect that shit, love yourself and move on with your life. To live your best life and go on doing the things that you want to do, while they sulk and feel neglected, because you aren't falling for their bullshit anymore. You have to learn the motto "not my problem". It will come in handy many times when dealing with the narc.

As long as you don't fear for your physical safety, you can live a somewhat normal lifestyle, with a brooding narcissist. I have learned that once they realize that there is nothing they can do to get under your skin, they will even back off a little bit. Some might even lose interest and leave you alone entirely. You don't have to "nag". You don't have to go to couple's counseling. You don't have to threaten them with divorce. Just ignore them. They hate not being the center of attention. You can derail their mental "game train" once you know what you are doing.

You need to keep reminding yourself that they are sick individuals that have used their narcissism to cope during a traumatic period in their life. It is a learned coping mechanism that they taught themself to survive. And even though your human instinct is to feel sorry for them and show them sympathy, you just can't. They are inhumane control freaks, and there isn't anything you can do to fix them. Nothing. After living with a narc for some time, you become accustomed to their behavior. I have come to learn that even if you did leave, chances are, you are going to leave one narcissist, just to fall into the arms of another. And not just because we are damaged goods, but because, just look around! Seriously, they are everywhere! The people you work with. Your parents, or maybe another member of your family tree. The friendly people you see every day at your local watering hole. That sweet little old man, who comes in every day with a joke and a smile, may very well be a narcissistic asshole in the privacy of his home. These types of people have more than one personality and are usually showing their best behavior when out in the public eye. So, it is impossible to think that we can cut out **every** narcissistic person we know, out of our life. Not without moving to the moon, anyway. So, if you don't have the resources to get away and start a new life at this very moment in time, you can still learn to embrace the life you have made for yourself, while unarming the narc, by learning how to play their game.

This book isn't to tell you that you have no other choice but to stay. I write this in the hopes that it opens your eyes, so that maybe you can spot them in the very beginning of a budding romance and get out, before there is too much invested. I also hope to give you options. Getting you to the point where you aren't as affected, or damaged by their actions, or words. Don't be mistaken, their actions and words will still sting from time to time, but you will quickly learn to bounce back with minimal scarring. Will this work for everyone? A big fat NO! But it worked for me, so far, and it just may be worth a second look. I can now spend more time concentrating on the things I deem important in my life, and less time contemplating on what tricks they are going to pull out of their sleeve next. Who cares! Let them throw their immature tantrums. Once again, not your problem.

Remember, the covert narcissist doesn't want others to see their true colors. They won't blow their cover and create too big of a scene in any situation. They don't want anyone to see them in a negative light. They want all the praise and attention that people can give them. They want to remain stealthy and save their unruly behavior just for you. But if you aren't always available for them, and can create a busy lifestyle for yourself, chances are they won't get to sabotage your plans as much as they'd like to. Start surrounding yourself with people. Make sure you have an extra set of ears and eyes that are always listening and witnessing when you interact with each other. Does this mean less free time for yourself? I hate to say it, but yes. The narc loves to get you alone, so there is no one around to witness his evil ways. Limit your "alone" time with the narc. They feed off it. One-on-one time is what they crave. They want to isolate you from your family and friends, so that they have you all to themselves. It's a trap. Fill your calendar with events. Fill your home with family and friends any chance you have. I can guarantee that they will hate it.

Make sure you put out the best possible self you can be, so that others notice your calm demeanor and goal-oriented lifestyle you have created for yourself. Touch everyone around you with your good vibes. Live in such a way, that when the narc tries to slander you, no one will believe them. Best revenge ever!

They will try anything they know how to do, to get you to come around to their way of thinking. And if they can't, they will rely on their power to recruit others and form their own posse, to use against you. This is where true friendships are a must. Because he will go directly to your closest friends first. If you have friends that like to talk shit behind your back, he will know to gather those for sure. They will be his favorites. The narc loves to recruit people whom you love and trust. But they will also, gladly befriend the very people that you have come right out and told them you dislike. They will do this, not because they really want to be friends with these people, but because it shows others that they can easily have a good relationship with them, so it must be something you are doing wrong. Clever huh? I have learned most of their tricks!

I can whole heartily admit that I am no longer ambushed by their actions. I can almost predict what they will say and do, before they even think of it. Once you get to know their game, you take away their power. Removing their shock factor, and the element of surprise from their arsenal, has become a lifesaver for me.

Rule number one when dealing with the narcissist, "Expect **the unexpected, without expecting too much**." That's easy enough, right? Or is it? They will purposely do or say something to get on your last nerve. If you have shown them any feelings of being frustrated or overwhelmed, you can expect it. They will come up with the darndest things just to trigger you. And when you finally can't take it any longer and lose your shit, they will happily point out your lack of control and call you crazy. They will tell you that you are overreacting and convince you that you have anger issues. Or my personal favorite...you're psycho! So, what do we do? Nothing! Keep your composure. No response is the worst reaction you can give them. It can be very comical and right down hilarious! The look on their face, as you silently turn away from them. Priceless!

So, how about we join forces and do this together! Let's dig in and find out what makes the narc, a narc? Let's turn the tables and pull all of the tricks out of their bag and expose them for what they really are. Just smoke and screens. There is nothing magical about them, at all. In reality, all a narcissist is, is someone afraid of solitude and change. They don't want anyone smarter, or more experienced, in anything, than they are. That would make them look "dumb" to others. They are afraid of abandonment. They brainwash you into thinking they are all you will ever need in this life, so that you will never leave them.

Because on their own, they have no power. They need people. They will seek them out like a tiger on the hunt. They can't wait to be the savior who brings you back to life with their magical ways. Their charm. Their generosity. Their all-knowing advice. And most importantly, their so-called "love". They will be delighted to pull you out of your funk and then expect you to spend the rest of your life at their feet, thanking them and trying to repay them for their act of kindness. Sickening!

We can wish all we want, to rewind the clock and go back and do things differently, but there are no do-overs. You have to decide if you even want to put forth the effort it will take in staying. Trust me when I tell you that the decision to leave them is no easy task either. So, let's read on and learn the realities involved, before we make our decision.

Let's just look at the honest facts presented to us. No fantasies of what could be. No temporary band-aids. No expectations. No measures taken, in trying to fix them. Just the cold hard facts. You got yourself into this without anyone's help. Now, it's your job to survive with the way things are or get out! Again, if there are any dangerous or violent acts committed against you, this is not for you. You need to take the steps needed to escape your abuser, for your own safety.

This book is solely for those that have grown accustomed to the mind games and can see past the fake personalities and delusional distractions. This is for those who decide they don't want to uproot their lives, or their children's lives, and be bullied out of their home. They have chosen not to abandon the way of life that they have made for themselves. This book is for those that want to gain control of their situation and possibly make it a little easier on themselves, until they have the ability to leave.

It could be because of financial stability, your children's needs, or the need to be near family members. Maybe you love your job, your friends, your home, and you just decided that you have too much invested to just walk away. Whatever the reason you have for staying, I will not judge you for it, because I have stood in your shoes. And so have many others. Don't let the "enablers" talk you into doing something that isn't right for you. They are not you.

Leaving the narc isn't always the cure for your problem either. Sometimes you can't make it go away by just saying good-bye. Chances are they will always find a reason to be in your life anyway. We can't rely on them just going away on their own. So, even if you do find a way to escape, they will most likely pop up again in your life somewhere down the road. Especially if you have children, or shared friends together. It's always nice to be prepared. And that is what I hope to do with this book. To help to prepare others on what to expect when staying with the narcissist. Knowledge is power. And power is what you want to take back for yourself.

CHAPTER TWO

Get Your Shit Together

When living with the narc, you will learn that the more you talk, the less they will listen. Things will change drastically during your first year with them. For you see, in the beginning, they are so talented with their word vomit and love bombing, that it is hard not to fall completely head over heels in love with the well-rehearsed narc. They all deserve an Oscar award for their performances. They will be the most attentive partner that you have probably ever known. They will hang onto every word that exits your mouth. They will remember your favorite foods. Your favorite song. Your favorite color. They remember all the little things that light up your world. They will soak up all this information, like a sponge, and store it in their closet of tricks. They insist on wanting to know everything about you. Including all your past relationships. How you get along with family members. All your worries and your darkest fears. Your dislikes. They want it all. And they will remember it all, to use against you at a later date. Not nice, but it's the truth.

One would think that you could trust someone who tells you that they love you. But, we all know, that is not always the case. Some people will feed off of your love for them. Like a parasite. And once they know that they have you where they want you, they will gradually become less and less interested in anything that you have to tell them. They will just stop listening. You will

find yourself repeating yourself over and over again. Do yourself a favor and just save your breath. They remember. They can hear you. They just choose not to acknowledge what you are saying. Your needs no longer matter to them. You are specifically in their life to please and satisfy their needs now. To heed their advice and do whatever they think is best for you, in order to serve them better. They no longer care what makes you happy. It's all about them. It always was, but you missed that part. They just tricked you into thinking that they took an interest in everything about you, so that they could snag you in their trap. Their "love" trap.
In knowing this, and being able to maintain your sanity, you must learn to pick your battles. Because in their eyes, you will never win the battle anyway. The more you express your feelings of disdain, the less they will acknowledge your feelings. The more you complain, or what they like to call it, "bitch", or "nag", the more they will make you feel needy, never satisfied, and completely batshit crazy. So just stop giving them what they want. Because not only will they tell you that you are crazy, but also the people you love and trust. Such as close friends, work relations, or family members. They love to go to **your** people and tell them all the slanderous details of your relationship. Nothing is sacred to them. But they will do it in a way that comes across as seeking their help in the matter. They will play the victim and act as if they have no one else to turn to. It's bullshit! They know exactly what they are doing. They can't wait to go behind your back and slander your name to those closest to you. They will say anything they can to make you look like the perpetrator instead of the victim. They will lie and make up horrible stories,

then quietly laugh at the reactions it brings. This is where it is extremely important to remember, that people who genuinely love you, do not go behind your back and purposely disrespect you.

As I said earlier, the covert narcissist is meticulously careful about what others see and hear. They are always on their best behavior when in the public eye. Only you will witness their "true colors." They will go out of their way to make sure that their stories match up with their actions. For they wouldn't want to look like a hypocrite, or a liar. They will remain so squeaky clean in the public eye, that when you speak negatively to anyone about them, they surely will not believe in what you are telling them. For they have never seen such behavior come from them. The narc will put on an award-winning act, as if they love your family and friends, as much as you do. They love it when your closest friends and family start to trust and befriend them. They will use their new friendships as weapons against you, if needed. They will specifically add them one by one to their so-called "posse", so that even if you were to leave, they will still have them in common with you. That will be the attachment that they need, to squeeze back into your life. Remember, they are sick and twisted. But this is where you are going to start fighting back.

This is where you are going to turn the tables. You are going to start matching your actions to your words. You are going to speak and act in such a way, that everyone around you will only believe you emit good vibes and shit sunshine. You are going to be the hardest worker in the room. You are going to be the most approachable. The most trustworthy. You are going to be the person that seems to have their shit together. This has to be your greatest performance ever! Whatever you do, do not let your guard down and act out in anger, or desperation. You cannot lose your composure. You have to fake it, at least, when in the public eye. And it's going to be hard! But you need to put on a show, just as they do, in order to gain the respect of everyone around you. Especially those with whom he confides in. You need to be extremely careful on who you talk to, about anything. Live a private life and stop posting it all over social media. Stop making your life an open book for all to see. It needs to appear to be all sunshine and roses, as far as they are concerned. You might often feel alone, or, as if you cannot trust anyone. And that's normal. Because most likely, you can't. I'm sorry to say, but even your closest friends may be a wealth of information for the narc. The narc has a very persuasive personality and knows how to gain the trust of others. They fooled you, so why do you think they couldn't fool anyone else?

Whatever you accomplish, they will downplay. Concerns you have, will be unnecessary worries. Whatever your goal is, it will be unattainable. Are you getting the picture? They will purposely attempt to trigger you, because they know they can. They want a reaction. And the best revenge you'll have in your pocket, will be to give no reaction. Absolutely none.

I'll give you an example of no reaction. I remember one February; we were experiencing some extremely cold temperatures. And on this particular day, we helplessly watched while our water pipes froze completely up in our back bathroom. What used to be the back porch, with no insulation whatsoever, became a laundry room and bathroom, thanks to the previous owner. I tried, to no avail, to get the water running once again. Because, when living with a narcissist, it will always be your responsibility to maintain the household and everything in it.

Their lives are way too busy for this trifle crap. (Plus, they have no problem-solving skills anyway.) It will also be your fault, if anything isn't working correctly. Because, after all, it is your job to see to it that everything does. They **allow** you to live in this beautiful home, so it is **your** job to see to its every need. The day after our pipes froze up, he called me on his way to work and asked, "what is your plan in dealing with the frozen pipes?" Priceless. But instead of arguing the fact that it was "our" problem, I told him that I would take care of it. Because that is what you do. You can explain that it isn't your sole responsibility all you want, because in their twisted mind, it is. So, I proceeded to call up a handy friend of mine and asked for his help in the matter. He not only thawed us out but took the preventative steps in seeing that it never happened again. Such a dear sweet friend. Get yourself some dear and sweet friends. Especially mechanically inclined ones.

I later conveyed this information, via text message, to my housemate and received absolute silence. He ghosted me all day. And didn't mention it when getting home later. Not a thank you. No questions on what was done, or how I solved the problem. Absolutely nothing. As was expected. I already knew what he was going to do. Get over it. You will never receive credit, or positive feedback for anything you do. So, you just need to rely on your own pat on the back. Learn to realize your resourcefulness and many talents. Gratitude is one of our greatest gifts. Be thankful for your ability to face the challenges. Because gratitude doesn't exist in the narcissistic world. They are never thankful for anything. Because nothing is ever enough for them.

I knew what to expect. I held the power of my reaction. I didn't send him a barrage of texts or express my disgust towards his rude actions. I simply gave no reaction and went on about my day. And that's what you have to do. You just go on with your day. It is your responsibility to make great days for yourself. Fill them up with everything and everyone you love. Give yourself something to look forward to when you wake up every morning. Don't dwell on your shitty situation. Sure, it's there, but you have to put it behind you in order to see what's in front of you. You have no time to wallow in self-pity. You are in survival mode. As long as you have decided to stay with the narcissist, you have to accept the fact that they will never put forth any effort, whatsoever, into investing in your happiness. The narc will never hold themselves accountable for their abusive ways. It will always be your fault they acted a certain way or said something hurtful. Stop waiting around for an apology that you will never receive. Don't waste your precious time. Instead, concentrate on all of the blessings you do have in your life. They are everywhere. And none of them involve the person deliberately trying to sabotage your sense of worth. They don't want you to find any good in anything, except them. They are your blessing. Without them you would be nowhere in life. Also, complete bullshit.

So, in knowing all of this, we have to give them a taste of their own medicine. You will stop saying thank you for anything they may do. No more noticing and complimenting on their "greatness". For example, they may do the laundry, or take out the garbage, which, in fact, should be a shared chore in any household, but you will not commend them on their help. You will no longer notice. Just as they no longer notice anything you do.

Isn't it funny how they will watch you work around the house from sunup until sundown and make no attempt to lift a finger to help you. But they will most definitely turn any small task they do, into an act of greatness. They will expect to be praised for it. But don't you dare do it. Let it go completely unnoticed. Chances are they don't pitch in that often anyway, so who cares if they stop all together, because of your lack of praise. Don't ask them for help with anything. Turn-abouts are fair play. Pivot and shoot from the hip. Give them a taste of their own medicine. Granted, they will throw a tantrum and complain to others on how you don't notice their great deeds. But that will just make them look "needy" and "weak." See where I'm going with this? There is instant gratification when you stop giving the person trying to make your life miserable, the attention they crave. They rely on attention. They need recognition and for others to tell them how great they are, at all times. They are a God in their minds. But not in your world. You are the one you need to start giving all the credit to. You are unstoppable. You are the definition of strength. You are the problem-solver. You are your own hero, and you don't need them. You are just accepting your fate and allowing them to remain in your life, until you decide when to leave. You are not trapped. You have made the decision to stay. You remain in control and can leave at any time. You don't need their permission. You don't need anyone's permission. You never did.

Learning to be self-reliant is a must. You are going to be so self-reliant, that you will not depend on them for anything ever again. And that will bother the shit out of them.

In becoming this person, I must warn you, that the narc might possibly lose all interest in you and move on to someone else. If this is what you are hoping for, then congratulations! The narcissist thrives on weaknesses. They can't compete with strength. Chances are, they found you at a very weak moment in your life. They preyed on your fears and vulnerability. Once you stop feeding them, they will hunt somewhere else. Or one can only hope.

The main goal in all of this is to gain back your power over your life. You will no longer look for the reaction of the narc. You will not ask for their advice. You will no longer ask for their approval. You won't even consider their opinion on anything that you decide to do for yourself. That's right... YOURSELF! Don't worry, because they will notice. They will accuse you of not "needing" them anymore. And they will be right. You won't. Let them adjust to that change, and once they are sure that you can't be budged in your solidity, they will give you the space you need. Their ego needs more attention than what they are receiving from you, so on to the next victim.

CHAPTER THREE

Expect Nothing

Earlier in chapter one, I commented on the number one rule when dealing with a narcissist. And that rule is, **"Expect the unexpected, without expecting too much."** That means that you have to put to rest all of the fantasies of them miraculously becoming the person they once were in the very beginning. That was all fake. Quit daydreaming of romance. Stop begging for empathy. Expect nothing, because that is exactly what you will get from them.

You see, in most relationships, two people can communicate their needs to one another, and most times, we will try their best to tend to these needs. That's because when two people genuinely love each other, they willingly show they care. They are not "forced" to do so. They don't keep score. They grow to love everything about each other. All of the quirky ways that make us who we are. That's what love is. It is enjoying each other's company. Becoming each other's best friend in life. It takes sacrifice, and not always getting your way on everything. It's taking the time to learn what the other appreciates, or dislikes, so as to not offend them.

Now, let's see what the narc does in a "relationship." They listen to your needs and do nothing. Or worse, they do the exact opposite of what you want. When you express your unhappiness, they accuse you of overreacting. You are just expecting too much.

They will gladly label you "needy" for wanting something. They will point out everything they have done for you, and how you still want more from them. Guaranteed, if you stay, they will spend the rest of their life committed to driving you completely insane and convincing you that you are hard to please, or worse, impossible to love. They will tell you that no one else could ever put up with you. They will remind you, again, of how lucky you are that they stay. Don't be fooled. This is what gaslighting looks like. It is their number one weapon that they rely upon, to twist everything around on you.

The narcissist doesn't know how to love. They only care about their ego. But do they love themselves? I'm not sure that they do. My belief is that they loathe themselves. They find it impossible to love anything in their life. They are only interested in their needs and will do anything to obtain whatever makes them seem happy. Even though they are not. In their eyes, they are convinced that they are showing you love, but you just can't see it. It's the best they can do. All bullshit! They don't want to change into who you long for them to be.

By not expecting them to express love, in a normal and rational way, you'll solve a lot of future problems that will pop up. Instead of jumping through their hoops, why don't you shower your family and friends with your love. Don't even waste your precious time proving your love to the narc. Because they don't care if you love them, or not. As long as you stay where they think they have you trapped, they will be content. They just want you to play out everything they require of you and to just be satisfied. Don't rock the boat. They are the captain of the shit ship, and you should be "thankful" that they are allowing you to sit in their boat. Hilarious!

To help ease the pain and heartbreak, you need to start expecting less and less from them. You need to stop relying on them for emotional support. Stop asking for financial support. You need to stop going to them for help of any kind. Every time you ask anything of them, even if it's a small task, or errand, they will make it seem like it is a daunting chore. They will constantly remind you of their good deeds and how they are here to "help" you. Do yourself a favor and get yourself a close friend who will gladly help you when needed. Having someone handy and mechanically knowledgeable is golden. Teach yourself how to do things. Become an expert in whatever field it is you need assistance in. YouTube is a wealth of knowledge. Learn to budget your money. Secretly, start saving your emergency fund. Learn to rely on yourself and be your own savior.

Most of us are taught at an early age that the one we give our heart to, will complete us. Our soulmate will complement our life by just being in it. They will shower us with their undying attention and gladly see to our happiness. This is how we are brainwashed as children. We see it in the happily-ever after movies we watch. We hear it in the once upon a time stories we read as a child. We spend our adolescence daydreaming of the "one". Then, we become adults and actually run into "the one", who is everything we have wished for. Who at first, is dripping with charm and charisma. They make a damn good first impression. Oh, I'm sure there are plenty of red flags thrown everywhere but are hidden by passion and sex. Our raging hormones can easily play tricks on us. The endorphins released are the enemy. They literally erase all logic and reason. I have learned that if you take sex out of the equation, you will see exactly what you are left with.

For some, sex isn't front and center. It is the friendship that you share with the other person that matters most. It's the things you find in common. It's the fun you have when you are together. The safe feeling you hold in your heart. But with the narc, sex is usually all they have to contribute. And they are more than likely good at it. They will demand physical satisfaction in return, for everything they do for you. You "owe" it to them.

They don't care if you hold hands, or not. They don't need dinner and a movie to get them in the mood. They don't need to dance to your favorite song. They don't care if you go all day without talking. They don't care how many times they hear "I love you." They only care about the sex. You could be angry at each other, and they will still want sex. They will tell you that you shouldn't go to bed mad. Telling someone how they should or shouldn't feel is called "gaslighting." It is their signature move. You could be ill, or exhausted from fatigue, and guess what...they will still want sex. They don't care how you feel, or why you feel that way. They need their physical needs met. They will make you feel as if you are "frigid" or callous if you don't give it to them. They will accuse you of using sex as a weapon, by withholding it from them. They will use these same accusations to have affairs and then turn around on you to justify them. If you decide to remain with the narcissist, you will either have to have a continual sexual relationship, no matter how they act, or expect them to find it elsewhere. I personally don't care anymore. I will not allow anyone to touch me that does not respect me. Let them leave. But when you make the decision to stay, you need to be aware of the likelihood of them having sexual affairs with others. Justifiably so, of course.

This is where it gets tricky. Because if they have an affair, that means they blow their image of an attentive and faithful partner. And you'd think this would be detrimental in their case, but it isn't. The narc has brainwashed everyone around you into thinking that they have been trying their best. They have openly expressed how they have exhausted every avenue and still can't get you to come around to showing them any intimacy. They will even have people defend their unfaithfulness. And guess what? Yes, you are still to blame. You will hear how it was all your fault that they couldn't remain faithful to you.

News flash! Couples who are in a loving and nurturing relationship, where they feel safe, want sex. They are naturally drawn to each other physically. They want to touch and show affection towards each other. So, if someone isn't wanting sex, then there must be something going on that we don't know about. There is abuse. Whether it be psychological warfare or verbal taunting. Bullying. Gaslighting. Be aware, because no one truly knows what goes on behind closed doors. If the lack of intimacy is so great of a problem, then why don't they just end the relationship? Why sneak around? We live in a free world. Get a damn divorce and go about your life.

I will never defend another who is unfaithful in a relationship. But when choosing to stay with a narcissist, this usually ends up happening. Even if you have a sexually active relationship with them. They will remind you of how you can always be replaced. Because "there are people out there just waiting to take your place". Someone as great as themselves, cannot be "wasted" on just one woman. At least that's what they make you believe. Completely sick and twisted.

So, in making a decision on whether to stay or not, you need to ask yourself if you can have sex without emotion? Can you have sex without affection? Without respect? Can you allow it to be physical and nothing else? I find the only two reasons a narcissist will stay in a relationship are money, and sex. They don't want to share or lose their money. And as long as the sex is there, they don't need much else. If you are willing to sacrifice your needs, so that theirs can be met, then more power to you. I wish you luck. Otherwise, start making more money.

We cannot predict our future. And it is hard to live in a cold and loveless world with the person we choose to spend our life with. But love is blind. At least until we open our eyes. We are not meant to live in a battle of wits and manipulation. We are not meant to beg for the affection of another. We are not here to stroke egos and fix everything they can't. Go back to when you were young and believed everyone to be fair and good. Forgiving and compassionate, as you are. That moment in time when you thought everyone you loved, would make you feel content and safe. Now it is your job to rewrite your ending. Your shell has to become just a little bit harder. You have to let go of all expectations. You are in the thick of it now, and nothing will ever go back to what it once was. As sad and defeating as that sounds, you need to rewrite your "fairytale" by learning to fall in love with your ability to love others, including yourself. Just because he/she doesn't love you, does not mean that you are not lovable. Start relying on yourself to make your own happiness. Bask in it. You have made this world bearable by not believing anything the narc tells you. You can't believe anything. It is all lies. Once you realize this, it is easy to listen to their criticism and damnation speeches of how they know what's best and you had better listen, or else. Nothing they say is true. They make it all up just to get their way. It's part of the game.

By expecting nothing, you can soften the disappointment of promises broken. By expecting nothing, you can help ease the heartache and ignore those feelings of insignificance. In knowing that you will not receive the praise, recognition, admiration, or respect for anything that you may do, you have already become more powerful in your situation. Your peers and family will notice all of your gifts and what you bring to the table. Who cares if he/she doesn't. You are not that same person who relies on their reaction. You will do things because you want to do them. You are no longer looking for validation. Because you already know it isn't needed in this new world that you have created for yourself. A safe place. A place where you have learned what to expect. A place where you can narrate their little verbal games word for word. A place where you don't solely rely on the love of the narc. Because, you know you are loved by others. You can create a place where you can express yourself anyway you choose. A world where you can freely contribute your talents, despite the naysayers that taunt you with their words of failure, within the walls of your home. You have the ability to love your life and find your self-worth. You will no longer allow yourself to be shaken by the insecurities of the narcissist in this life you have re-created for yourself.

CHAPTER FOUR

The Power of Silence

Remember how it was, in the beginning, of pretty much every relationship you have ever been in? Remember all the conversations where you would happily stay up all night just to text, or discuss every little thing that popped into your head? Well, it is safe to say that those days are probably long gone. Enjoy the memories. All those conversations that made us giggle and squeal with delight are gone. The playful banter that took place, that was once arousing, is also gone. All normal reasoning and common sense are no longer found. They have been replaced with "I am right, and you are crazy for thinking that way."

I used to think that if two people could not easily communicate with one another, then the relationship would surely be short-lived. I was wrong. As I grew older, I started studying couples that had been together for twenty or more years. I started to notice how they would hardly ever look at one another, let alone speak to each other. I would see them enter a restaurant, and literally, the only words spoken were when they placed their order. They would eat their whole meal without looking up from their table setting. I had always thought, how miserable they must. It was only later in life, that I finally began to realize that sometimes conversation is overrated and can kill the mood. Too much talk can be fatal, when dealing with a narc, and silence is golden. Most of the time we find ourselves spewing some mindless chatter just to hear ourselves talk, because we feel anxious, or nervous. Being in the same room with the narc, we may feel that we have a responsibility to fill up every empty space with noise because the awkward silence is deafening. We don't want them to concentrate on their next move, so we talk without intent. We mindlessly spew out anything just to have a conversation. I have learned, the hard way, that my greatest relationships were those where I felt content to say nothing. Where I didn't feel anxious or pressured into a conversation. I was able to relax in silence and still feel connected to the person next to me.

I now wish I could take back every spoken word that left my lips in desperation. All with whom I wasted my precious energy just to "make things easier" on them. Too much talk has always led to disagreements and arguing. I'd find myself defending my decisions made. Disclosing my deepest secrets. Forcing my opinions. Who the fuck cares and why do they need to know? To this day, I still hate talking on the phone with someone longer than five minutes. I'm sure it is a trauma response learned from the past. But I find the longer you talk, the more it just leads to gossip and negativity. Blurting out things that ought to be kept unspoken. I don't want any part of it. So, in dealing with the narc, why would you even think that you need more conversation to make your relationship work? What do you think is going to happen? Do you really believe that they will respect your view on anything you have to say? You should probably stick to talking about the weather, or what you plan on making for supper. Those are the only safe topics to chat about. One would think anyway. Better yet, try not to talk to them at all. I'm serious! I have tried to stimulate my brain cells by talking about current events. Politics. A newspaper article that I had read. A book, or a movie I was interested in, and immediately regretted it as soon as the words left my mouth. A narcissist cannot process how someone else feels about something, because they only care about how they feel. So do yourself a favor and keep your mouth shut. You can't expect someone who doesn't look past their own nose, to be aware of anything of importance going on around them. They love the chance to make you feel like an idiot. Why would you give them the ammunition they need?

They will purposely never agree with you on anything. You say black and they will say white. They will debate with you until you are blue in the face and are forced to leave the room for your own sanity. They already know how you feel about it. They already know your views and opinions. Remember, you are their favorite subject. They studied you and memorized your every word and actions in the beginning stages of your relationship. They know what makes you tick and what makes you explode with anger.

They will deliberately go out of their way to agree with someone that they know you cannot tolerate. They will loudly praise those particular people that you don't have any respect for. They will openly bring up subjects that they know will trigger you. Stop allowing them to have any say on anything. Who cares? No reaction is a reaction. The words that are purposely spoken to trigger you...ignore. The demeaning comments spoken under their breath...ignore. Why is it so important for you to have these conversations, when you know how it is going to end? You don't need to be right! Let them think however they choose to think. Stay tight-lipped as possible. Better yet just walk away. Stop giving away your power.

You need to keep busy with activities that bring you joy. Find a hobby. Find something to occupy your time. If it gets you out and away from the narc, even better! At least then you will have some peace in your life. Sitting around looking at each other all day is not going to end in your favor. You need a reason to keep as far away from them as possible. Get a part-time job. Go workout at a gym, or travel. Get outside. Do something you love that doesn't include them. The less chance you have at having conversations, the better. Don't even sit in the same room with them while they are watching the news. I learned this right away. They will use the daily news as a reason to bring up a subject they know you will lose your shit on. It thrills them with delight to see you squirm with disgust. Take yourself out of the equation. Problem solved. As far as they are concerned, you have no opinions on anything. You just don't care. Save your "talk time" for close friends. Debate with those you know to be open-minded. Read in private. Have a place you can go and let down your guard and actually be at peace with yourself.

You will start to enjoy your solitude. Enjoy the time spent alone. It can be heaven, when living with a narcissist. The only heaven you will experience. Learn to trust your decisions without needing an opinion from another. Learn a craft, or how to repair something, so that you no longer need their assistance. Save some money and budget your finances, so that you don't have to sit through the lectures every time you ask for money. Give them little, or no reason, to feel important, or needed in your life. That is all they want. To feel as if you couldn't exist without them. They are depending on you to feed their huge ego. They want you to know how you would be helpless without their help. So quit asking for it.

Gather with your friends for conversation without him/her. Don't include them. No need to feel guilty about it, because they don't give a shit anyway. Most narcissists, I have met, have little need for friends. They feel that friends are just a waste of time, unless of course we are talking about your friends. Trust me. They don't need an opportunity to bond with your friends. That would be a horrible mistake. Believe me when I say, they will use your friends to manipulate you into getting what they want. Or, in getting the information that you don't want them to know about. The narc uses people. Stop giving them the opportunity to get what they need.

Learn to spend time with yourself. Living with them is hard enough without putting yourself through the forced "friendship" that will never develop. You don't have to spend every waking moment together with anybody. Especially the narcissist.

Live as if you are single. Live as if you live alone in your home. If you want to remain under the same roof, you need to act as if they aren't even there with you. I know, it sounds ridiculous! But, it is a must, in order to accomplish anything. Don't share your future plans with them. Don't ask permission for anything. Don't ask for help with any problem that may pop up during your day. Don't include them in any get-togethers you create with your friends. And above all else, stop thinking that you can have a normal conversation with them. Because you can't! You need to be self-sufficient and independent in every way possible in order for this to work.

You are not in a normal relationship. You need to accept this fact. The narc is not on your side. They do not want what is best for you. They only want what is best for them. And you having your own opinions and making your own decisions, without their help, is going to drive them crazy! They will try to shut you down before you even get started. So, keep it to yourself. They won't have the chance if they have no insight on what you are doing. Your life doesn't need them as a cheerleader. Learn to trust yourself. That is how you become self-reliant. It will be your greatest weapon of defense when living with the narc.

CHAPTER FIVE

Always Have an Escape Plan

In other words, don't get too comfortable. Because you will learn that the narcissist is unpredictable and will change their mind at any time. One day it's all sunshine and roses, and the next, all hell will break loose. Mood swings, that they will never admit to. The silent treatment, the tantrums, and all because everything is your fault. They seem to think that they hold all the power. That they are the only living creatures entitled to emotions of resentment, hate, and jealousy. But you absolutely cannot express any disdain or dislike about anything, at any time. "If you don't like it, there's the door." "You can leave at any time." Well, yes, I can. But as soon as I reach for the doorknob, you turn into a crumbling pile of "why can't I make you happy?" bullshit. I get to hear about all the things you have done for me but still don't appreciate you. I get to hear everything you have sacrificed to make our relationship work. How I'll never find another like you. God...I should hope not! You are, hopefully, a one-of-a-kind special that I wish not to repeat in life.

Start planning a backup plan and keep a bank account full of emergency money he knows nothing about. Keep a suitcase packed with essentials hidden away in a closet. Make sure you have good credit; in case you need to get an emergency loan.

You are in charge of your well-being. And it is up to you to save yourself! You, and only you, will know when enough is enough. You are the only one going through the secret hell at home. Ignore the opinions of others that think your man is an angel put on this earth and how any other person would be lucky to have your life. All the comments on how you have it "so damn good and need to count your blessings". They only see what the narcissist wants them to see...all the good. But you know the truth and have the power to get out. It is your decision on whether you stay or leave.

You owe no one an explanation. The narc will play dumb but will know exactly why you left. He needs to play the victim. Don't waste your breath on unnecessary explanations, that you have had on repeat, for years now. The narc doesn't care. But keep in mind that they will happily put on a show and invite everyone to their pity party. Let others think exactly what they want to think. Not your problem. Just because they believe it, doesn't mean it is true. You have more important things on your plate at the moment, than to be involved with idle gossip, finger pointing, and hearsay, that they know nothing about.

The most important thing when living with the narc, is that they can, and will pivot without a minute's notice. They will turn the tables upside down with a plot twist, and it will be all on you. You are the reason for their fits of rage. You are the reason things have changed, for the worst, in the relationship. You are the one who needs to figure it out. But what they are oblivious to, is that you already have. You have been planning your escape since the day you finally opened your eyes. You know exactly what to expect. You have been planning for the unexpected and you will be ready for it when it happens. You need to start keeping secrets. Even from your besties. The less people know, the better it will be.

I know how hard it is to go through life being your own hero. For your own safety, you can't depend on anyone. People are fickle. They are your friend one day and talking shit behind your back the next. You honestly can't completely trust anyone. Not even family members, to have your back at all times. The narcissist knows exactly who to go to first, in times of trouble. That's right...your family and closest friends. The people you always believed to be in your corner cheering you on. The ones that promised to be there for you in your time of need. The blood that is "thicker than water." The narc will hit them up first with his slanderous tales of woe, then act all desperate to do whatever it takes to help mend the relationship. They will delightfully rely on their pity. They'll pretend to need advice and direction. Don't think it doesn't work, because it does! They are masters at deceit. More than once, I have been in a situation, where I kept silent about what was going on, and to my surprise, I was approached by a family member, or friend about the subject. They knew about what was going on, longer than I realized. The narcissist doesn't waste any time. They will seek out and gather their posse, almost immediately, at the first sign of trouble. They cannot risk being implicated as the "bad guy" in all of this. They need to tell their side of the story before you get to speak up with your version.

Gossip is a must-have in a narc's life. They thrive on it. They can't wait to hear all the bad and inconvenient circumstances that someone else is experiencing. They get their "rocks off" on this type of information. They surround themselves with informers, and people that do nothing but talk shit about others. They live for it and store it in their arsenal for their future needs. The more they know, the more power they hold in damaging someone else's life. For that is their sole purpose on this earth. To destroy and conquer. You'll see the gossipers all huddled somewhere in an intimate conversation, whispering their versions of what "really" happened. Most times, they will place themselves in a one-on-one conversation with someone you once considered a friend, but found out they liked to talk too much, so detached from their friendship.

The hard reality in living with a narc, is that the very same person you fell in love with, is the same person you are now trying to survive with or escape from. How did it get like this? Why did you allow this to happen to yourself? You knew from the very first time they displayed their toxicity, that you should have turned and run, but were too blind with false feelings to see the exit sign. What's worse, is that you probably thought you could change them and "love" all the bad away. That if you stayed with them long enough, they would start to see all the chances that you had given them, and how you continued to love them through it all, despite all their bad behavior. That one day, they would miraculously realize all the love you have given them and freely give it back to you... FAT CHANCE!

That is not how it works. They see their many "chances", or "do-overs", and don't care how many more they will get. They are happy because you are willing to put in the work and they don't have to do shit. You are the one who keeps falling off the bicycle. You are the one who continually needs to get back on and jump through the fiery hoops in this circus that you have created for yourself. Not them. You are the main event. They are so phenomenally great, that you will continue to find ways to give them a fresh start. Another chance. Why can't we see that they are the ones that have us acting all crazy. We are delirious in thinking it will ever work with a narcissist. Because they aren't losing any sleep over analyzing any situation. They aren't feeling remorseful, because of something they might have done wrong. They honestly feel they should not have to put forth any effort, whatsoever, into making anything in their life better. That is your job. They are faultless and "deserve" a second chance from you. They demand explanations on why you acted as you did, over something they said. They will convince you that it must be your insecurities that have caused them to look like the perpetrator in all of this. They insist on you, examining your own mental health, and heal yourself, so that you stop feeling as though they are the enemy in your relationship. Don't even flirt with the idea, or eventually you will end up losing your mind.

The narc does not deserve the extra time and attention that they think they deserve. They do not deserve the counseling, or therapy that they will deceitfully suggest, in trying to save the relationship. Stop circling around the center ring on your unicycle. Their ego is just going to grow even larger, than it already is, when they see the extra steps, you are willing to take, just for them. Why do you feel you have to do more? Haven't you already done everything that you could possibly do?

Have you ever heard the phrase "It takes two to tango?" That it "takes two" to make or break a relationship? I say bullshit! That's just some somebody's way of wanting you to think that you haven't gone through enough obstacle courses, in trying to repair your broken relationship. The truth is, that sometimes you do all you can, and it still doesn't work. I say, couples that have endured many years of hardship usually involve an equation of one producing all the shit, and one putting up with all of it.

Why should I give credit to someone who has done everything in trying to destroy my self-confidence and any "love", or feelings, I have been trying to hold on to for all these years? They don't deserve to be included in my survival story. I did all the work. I am the reason there is still a "relationship", if that's what you want to call it. It starts and ends with me. I allowed it. Now it all depends on whether I want to continue with this sham, or call it quits and go on with my life. Why should I include them in my dance? They haven't put in any fruitful effort. They haven't experienced their sanity slowly leaking out of them, or seen their world turn into a twisted version of "normal".

My advice to anyone dealing, living with, or in love with a narcissist is, that you need to start doing less and less, and start giving yourself more and more. More credit, for everything you have tried to do, up until now. You have learned the hard way. The only way there is, in finally realizing that there is absolutely no way in hell it is ever going to work. Ever. It is up to you on whether or not you can live without it. It is a choice that you, alone, have to make. And if you choose to leave, then do it quietly and deliberately. Don't look back with guilt. Prepare in silence and execute your plan when the time is right. Only you will know when enough is enough. Have faith and believe in yourself. You are in control of your destiny.

CHAPTER SIX

Embrace Your Strength

When you live with a narcissist for any length of time, you will start to feel insignificant. What else were we expecting? Naturally, this comes from years of brainwashing and gaslighting tactics that have been skillfully executed by the narc, who "loves" you. You can't totally blame yourself for feeling as if your life has no purpose, and you are just a major "fuck up". Or can you? After all, we have allowed the abuse to continue. We have accepted their behavior and have considered it the "norm". We include dysfunction and toxicity in our everyday life.

They want you to feel small and too tired to fight back, but in reality, you are made of amazing strength. You just haven't embraced it yet.

You have lived through some cruel and horrendous experiences. You are a survivor. It is time to show the world how strong you really are.

This will take a lot of inner strength and respect for yourself. In helping you get to this point of self-adoration; you need to start looking at yourself as if you are watching from the outside in. Pretend that you are peering through the window of your life and start observing what is really happening. What do you see? What do you see playing out before you every damn day of your life? It's not pretty, is it?

Would you allow your best friend, or a beloved family member, to live as you are living now? You would probably jump in and help them anyway you possibly could. Right? Well, why not learn to help yourself. Learn how to save yourself. To give yourself that extra boost in order to get out of the hole that you have found yourself in.

People seem to think that self-love should not be present in a thriving relationship. That you should selflessly give up everything you want and need, so that your lover, or "soulmate" has everything they need to be happy. That love is putting others' needs first. Big mistake. Jesus himself told his followers to love your neighbor as yourself. That implies that you need to love yourself, in order to love others properly.

Why are we expected to give up everything, including the fight inside us, for love? Stop! The reason you attracted the narcissist, in the first place, is most likely because you didn't show enough self-respect in the beginning of the relationship. You allowed red flags to be thrown everywhere without screaming FOUL or speaking up. You looked the other way, in the hopes that they would "change their ways" on their own.

Then when you felt it was probably too far gone to get out, you decided to stay and just deal with it. And dealing with it has wrung you dry. There is no more fight left inside. You have thrown up the white flag, just to have peace. I say, fuck that!

You need to get some thicker armor. You need to learn how to deflect the shit they keep throwing your way. You need to stop thinking about what they want. You've done everything you can think of to try and turn this around and failed. No one has ever beat a narc at their own game. Until now.

Take all your dreams of romance, love, and your wish upon a star bullshit, and burn it. Literally. Write everything you have ever wanted from the person you are bending over backwards for, on a piece of paper. Then go outside and dig a hole, light the paper on fire, watch it burn, then bury it. You are allowed to cry. Then be DONE! Rebirth is in the making. You are in the beginning stages of recreating the new person that no longer gives their power away.

No one can destroy your dreams. No one can distort the truth. No one can make you feel special. No one can change your world. You got yourself into this, now you need to muster up all the strength you have left and fight back. What are they going to do? Leave you? That would be a win/win situation. Because other than death, that is the only way you will be rid of them. When "they" make the decision to leave. You cannot rid yourself of them, just by deciding to end it. They will not let go, simply because you want them to. They have to make the decision to leave.

But in order to get them to dislike the taste of you in their life, you need to become resilient and positively in love with who you are. Find joy in life. Bask in the greatness of who you are. Smile. Laugh. Start involving yourself in things happening around you. Become friends with outgoing people. Do group events. Have house parties. Start more than one hobby. Become so active, that they can't get you alone to perform their hat tricks. The narc hates an audience when they want to be cruel. They look forward to one-on-one time to do that shit.

Become so comfortable in your own skin, that they start to look at you with disgust. (Insert snorting laugh here)

Strength and self-esteem are the two main ingredients in ending a relationship with the narcissist. They will gladly spit you out of their pitiful lives. And in the meantime, you will learn to love yourself again. You will see all you have to offer the world and not just one person. You weren't meant to just live for one person in the first place. You were brainwashed into thinking that way from all of the relationship "experts" that invited themselves into your personal life. You know, the ones that can't find happiness in their own backyard, so they feel the need to stick their nose in where it doesn't belong, with their unsolicited love advice and relationship hacks.

With all the help you receive from society, your family, and all the religious institutions, I'm surprised there is any difficulty in finding a true "soulmate" at all! It should be the easiest thing in the world to do! I mean look at all the experts out there! Ugh!

Listen, no one else will ever be you. No one else came from where you came from. No one else knows how you feel inside. No one knows what is best for you, except yourself. The problem is that you have been taught not to listen to your own needs. All you have to start doing is listen to that little voice inside your head, screaming "get the fuck away as fast as you can!" It's called survival and there is nothing "selfish" about your own preservation.

Times are changing. People are staying single longer. They have no immediate need in sharing their most intimate moments with another person. Oh, sure, there are still those who feel inadequate without someone clinging to their arm, but they are fewer than once was, and this makes me all giddy inside. We can finally go through life being secure in our singleness! We found we can survive without another's last name and not be looked upon with sympathy. Poor woman just never found her "soulmate". Hallelujah!

I can be confident, strong, bold, defiant, and unbending in my life decisions for me, myself, and I, and not be considered a selfish bitch. I no longer look over my shoulder to catch someone's reaction as I walk by. I sit in a crowd and no longer feel anxious or prompted to perform. I am finally whole! I put in the inner work to see how wonderfully and powerfully I could love myself just as I am. AS I AM. I can honestly say that I don't think anyone else could ever love me as much as I already do. I no longer care how others see me in their eyes. I am unaware of judgment, or whispers. I go through life as I wish. I wear what I want. I talk as I please, with no one there to silence me. And it is a wonderful feeling.

When you get to this point, you will be amazed at how freeing it is. But it takes time. The narc has turned you into someone who you don't even recognize. You no longer know what it is that you want for yourself, because they have spent years doing all the thinking and decision making for you. You have lived your life on autopilot just to keep the peace. You have silenced your inner child and stomped out all the dreams of what could have been, just to settle for the life you have now. The life that THEY want you to live. The life that makes THEM happy. You have been taught that when you love someone you live for them.

It will take months, and sometimes years, to get to the point where you just can't do it any longer. But believe me when I say, YOU WILL GET THERE! I remember the day, the hour, and exact moment I decided I had enough! It was like someone flipped the switch and you can bet I wasn't going to turn it back on anytime soon. I made the decision to get my shit together and get the hell out of my miserable life. I deserved better from myself. I needed to give myself the life I had always dreamed of. No one else was in charge of my happiness. I finally figured out the problem. It was me. I was an enabling, forgiving, second-chancing foo, who was giving the narc permission EVERY single day to treat me like shit and it needed to stop.

I can be happy alone. I can treat myself better than he could, so what in the hell was I doing? What was I afraid of?

Whatever you do, don't show fear. Fake it anytime you can. You cannot allow the narcissist to see your true feelings. And, I might add, that you cannot allow the narcissist's friends, or posse, see your true feelings. Remember, when you decide to live with a narc, your whole world is a false facade. A lie. You have to learn to smile on the outside, while dying on the inside.

CHAPTER 7

When You Just Can't Do it Anymore

I recently started the process of detachment. It took me 3 months to get the hell out, but I finally found my own place and moved on. But, as you already know, that doesn't mean I have escaped completely from my predator. The narc will never let go, unless THEY want to let go. They will use every excuse in the book to use the "meet up" and "let's talk" bullshit. Don't do it! Manipulation at its finest.

They will tell everyone around them how much they miss you and how you should give them "another" chance. Listen, you and I both know that you have given them every chance available, over and over again. Don't let your friends, family, or that stranger that knows way too much about your relationship, get to you. It is your decision to make, and by the sounds of it, you have made the correct choice for you.

The narc collects people. And some of the closest people you had in your circle will cross over to his side. It is a heart-wrenching process to witness, but it will happen. You will find yourself defending your decision to the very people that you thought had your best interests at heart. This is where you find out who is, or was, your true confidant.

You have every right to cut ties and let go, as painful as that may be. You can't have anyone around causing you to second-guess your chance at a new life. The hardest thing you will ever do in your lifetime, is to cut off the narc. You had to go through months, maybe years, of mental warfare and manipulation. You were the narc's emotional punching bag. You fed them what they needed every damn day. And now that you have finally made the choice to walk away, do you really think you need friends, or family members in your life tripping you and pulling you back along your journey? NO!

Get rid of all the unnecessary drama! Shelter yourself from all the nay-sayers and preachers of doom. Stay away from family functions, or gatherings where these people may be invited. Distance yourself from any event or place where they gather in numbers. I say that because where there is one, there will be others. Most of the time you are the favorite subject to talk about and everyone in the room will most likely know about your situation and want to chime in with words of wisdom. Just stay away. You need to be on your own with no distractions. Not even from the people who claim to love you.

Your new life is going to involve new hangouts. You can't expect change if you are still revisiting the shared watering hole that you and the narc would visit. You may even need a new job, new home, new town/city, and yes...new friends. Not "our" friends.

There are many factors to consider in leaving the narcissist. It isn't as simple as walking out the door. You have to carefully plan every step you take. You have to be aware of all the pitfalls that you will run into. The narc is going to make it just as hard to leave them as it was to live with them. Maybe, even harder. They don't like to lose...especially with an audience. Everyone is watching. Everyone is judging. People might think they are the asshole in all of this, and God forbid that happen!

If I had done it over again, I would have planned an extensive trip, or vacation and moved out, just before I went away. Get moved out and leave for somewhere beautiful and relaxing. Away from family, friends, and the narc. A month if you can. I know it is a lot, but the longer you are away from shared people in your life, the better off you will be in obtaining your freedom and peace of mind.

Make sure you are financially able to move out. The narc will not help you escape. You have to do it on your own. Start saving money, and don't breathe a word of your plan to anyone. ANYONE. The less people know, the more likely your goal will be obtained. Work in silence. Remember, it has to be an ambush. It has to come unexpectedly so that they cannot plan on their counterattack. Plan your move when they are at work, or on vacation. You owe them no explanation. They already know why you are leaving. Stop wasting precious energy on the same shit, over and over again. It is time to execute your plan and put it into action!

Look at all the tedious work you put into getting your life back. Take it seriously. Don't let your stupid emotions of guilt or your empathy for the narc's feelings stop you from your goal. There is a reason why this plan of action was planted in your mind. It didn't just happen. Something they said, or did, finally sparked that flame inside of you. Sometimes, after months, or years of psychological abuse, it takes that special moment, when you know that there is no earthly way you are going to put up with anymore of the bullshit. You just know. In a blink of an eye, everything changes. It is almost like you have finally come to your senses. A big slap in the face to bring you back to your reality.

Once this happens, there is no turning back. The dance with freedom has begun. It constantly grabs your hand and leads you out onto the dance floor of your life. You entertain the idea of leaving. You start to think about when and how you will eventually do this. You find yourself daydreaming of the mornings you can wake up in peace and quiet. You move in silence. Almost ashamed of these thoughts. But trust me...they are there for a reason and I like to call it survival.

I am here to tell you, that whatever your situation, you can, and will, one day get back the life you dream of, but you will never be the same as you were before living with the narcissist. You can take all the steps in healing your broken mind and soul, but you have lived through some of the most haunting and traumatic events of your life that will never be forgotten. And you should remember these dark times. Your memory serves you as a protective shield from repeating the same mistake again. More than likely, you will remain single for an extensive period of time. You will find it hard to trust yourself and others, when it comes to affairs of the heart. And that's fine. It is completely normal to feel "put off" when someone takes a romantic interest in you. You aren't ready yet. It is hard to say when you will be able to share your newfound solitude with another.

It took you so long to get to this point, that you will find it very hard to let it go. Does that mean a single life from here on out? For me it has. I have learned to love my own company and feel no need to make room for another any time soon.

It has been seven years, and counting, since I have been intimate with someone. I love the friendship of a man, but I cannot fathom sharing my life with one, ever again. Does this mean I haven't completely healed yet? Perhaps, but why is there something wrong with me, just because I wish to remain single? That's right...there is nothing wrong with that wish.

The narcissist will move on but torment you in secrecy. They will act like they have found a wonderful new life without you, but send that text, or purposely place themselves where you are, every chance they get. This is why you cannot share friends with the narc. They will use these friendships to their advantage to keep in touch with you and what you are doing. No contact. In any shape or form. None. As inconceivable as it may be, the person you believed to be incapable of being cruel, is now the monster living alongside you. Once you fall in love, it is harder to leave. But leave you must. And when you do, you cannot, under any circumstances, have any "friendly" contact. You cannot "meet up" for a chit chat. Stay away from them if you see them at an event. Don't mention their name to anyone ever again.

This personal history will be tragic and traumatic. It will be something that you will never forget. It will also be something that you will never want to repeat. Keep that in mind when dipping your toe into the future dating pool. Now that you know what to look for, don't fall into the same trap twice. Be careful with your heart. It is precious and breaks so easily. Treat your life as if you are caring for a dear friend or family member. Stop risking your happiness for some temporary fix. It is better to remain single, than to go back to where you just escaped.

CHAPTER 8

You Do Not Have To "Let It Go".

By now, you should have a realistic picture of how devastating life can be in dealing with a narcissist. I have touched on every nasty detail and have been brutally honest on where you stand in their life. The most repeated regret I have had in all of this, is the constant blame I put on myself for allowing their behavior, and wasting most of my precious life on surviving, and escaping the situation I put myself in. I willingly entered into the relationship, more than once, fully aware of how monstrous and unfeeling they could be, and told myself over, and over, that I could heal them with my loving forgiveness. I made every excuse in the book for them. From their rotten childhood to their past relationships for being the way they were. At no time did they ask for my forgiveness, nor made any attempt to change their behavior. They believed themself to be clear of all blame, and found no fault in their actions, or words. I allowed the narc to live as if they were perfect in every way. I put them up on the imaginary pedestal and masked all their faults, while painting them "perfect" for all to see.

I believe it is harder to forgive oneself, more than it is to forgive another. I carry the remorse and anger that has visibly changed my personality. I am not the same person that I was before the narc. I have become bitter towards "love" and affection. I am repulsed by the words. I no longer believe that I will ever find love again. Not that I am incapable, or undeserving of love, but because I no longer believe anything a man tells me. I see them as liars, who will say and do anything just to get you into their grasp. Their trap. I am afraid of intimacy and probably will be for the remainder of my life. This is one of the effects that you have to expect when living way too long with the narcissist. PTSD to be clinically correct. This aftershock will remain with you, possibly, forever.

I believe that when going through something traumatic, your body stores the trauma, as a safety measure, to remind you NOT to enter into the same situation again. I embrace my bitterness, for it has protected me from more than one bad decision out of loneliness.

The fear of living alone for the rest of my life, no longer daunts me. I expect it and welcome it. I will protect my peace at any cost.

I am not on repeat. I am amidst the process of rebuilding my life, and I will not revisit any situation that I have already experienced. I will not be a friend. I will not accept the invitation to a "friendly" get-together.

The narcissist will depend on you giving them every chance to get back into your life. They will wait for the allotted time period, before they ever so slightly poke their toe inside your door, in the hopes that enough time has gone by, to where the offenses don't seem as fresh and painful. Absence makes the heart grow fonder. Time heals all wounds. Yeah...NOT!

I regret all the times I walked back into the arena, where I got my ass kicked, without my armor. With a trusting smile and new love in my heart for the same perpetrator that committed horrendous crimes against me. Over and over, I allowed my heart to get crushed. I was like a hamster on a wheel. Same situation. Same outcome.

Did I receive any merit, or an award for such forgiveness? Where are my special bonuses in life for not giving up on the relationship, by allowing his abusive behavior? All I have to show for any of it, is a jaded heart, and an untrusting attitude towards anyone, who approaches me, with any thought of sharing my most sacred space that I have created for myself.

In my recluse, I have found creativity. In the quiet of the mornings, I have new hope in a new and rewarding future. I have time to plan. I can see happiness and fulfillment during the end years of my life. I no longer search for someone beside me in the still of the night. I no longer ache for the sound of someone breathing, or a heartbeat echoing in the darkness. For I am the light of my life. I am the one who brings kindness and respect to the table. I am my own savior. I have given myself a better life, by counteracting with grace. I did not lose my cool. I did not lose my mind. I did not lose myself during those painful years. I allowed myself the time needed to prepare my escape. I did not make hasty decisions that put myself, or anyone else dear to me, in an uncomfortable position.

I am a survivor. And you are gravely mistaken if you think I will risk my peace, to quickly jump back into another relationship. I have learned my lesson the hard way. And the hurt is a scar that reminds me of how good I have it now, and how not to relive any of it again. Pain is purposeful. It is there for a reason...to protect you. The dull ache that remains, brings you back to your senses. It is there to wake you up from your daydreaming in "make-believe" land.

The harsh reality is, when leaving a long-term relationship with a narc, you will have an everlasting scar on your heart and soul. It is there to remind you of the love that you poured out onto this hurtful person, over and over again, in order to try and convince them of how much you wanted them in your life. All the times you looked the other way, or made excuses for their actions, so they wouldn't look like monsters to others. You protected their reputations, as if they were your very own.

The pain is there to help you heal. If there is such a thing as "healing". I don't think I will ever heal, but I will not allow my pain to take front and center, as it once did. I will not be consumed in regret and sadness for all my fruitless efforts. I will not punish myself for all the mistakes I made with a loving heart. You have to learn to forgive yourself. But, by no means, are you required to forgive and forget. Hold on to the memories. Keep them as a constant reminder of how you need healthy boundaries in your life. Stop giving all of yourself away to others. You do not need to "just let it go", as the offenders will suggest.

Be wary of those who constantly make it your problem for not letting something go. These people are the type that rely on the art of you forgetting their offenses. How are they to repeat their crimes, if you hold them accountable for their actions? How are they to cross over those boundaries you create for yourself? I will no longer be chastised for feeling anger and hurt. Are we to become numb and unfeeling, just for the comfort of another? Am I expected to give them a "hall pass" and allow them to upset my peace? If I rebuke, or speak up in my defense, why does it become MY problem?

We should be allowed to feel what we feel. Just because someone says they are sorry; doesn't mean it will never happen again. It is our choice on whether to believe in their apology, or not. Instead of expecting someone to turn a blind eye, or the other cheek, we should encourage others to stand up for themselves. Not make them feel guilty or shamed for showing anger toward their offender. Stop enabling these ogres. Let's make them squirm with our healthy reaction, like they willingly make us squirm, while triggering us for their feeding frenzy. Forgive yourself. Whether, or not, you forgive them, is up to you.

Chapter 9

The Reverse Discard

By now, I hope that you have realized that the narcissist is very persevering when it comes to getting what they want. They are relentless in their efforts. But there will come a day when they grow tired of the chase and start to look for new supply.

When you become aware of their tactics and can name them, even before they use them, it won't be fun for them anymore. They cannot ambush when you are onto their next move. When they can no longer extract the reaction that they crave from their behavior...the party is over.

They will crave a new victim. Fresh blood, so to speak. Someone who is unaware of their covert personality. Someone easily charmed by their words, and appreciative of all their love bombing. That wouldn't be you any longer, so now they are "forced" to break it off, and move on. But, not without a smear campaign.

You put them in a position where now they have to cover their tracks and look like the victim to the others watching and listening. They cannot look like the monster that kicked you to the curb.

Reverse discard is where they make it so unbearable, you have no other choice but to get out. They will save this card for their last play of the game. This is only used when they know there is no longer a chance of reconciliation, or to win you over. Be prepared for some action. You will be known as the monster who abandoned them after "everything they had done for you". Remember, without them, you would be nothing.

Their posse will jump right on this, as expected, and join in the smear campaign. They will make sure they tell everyone around them how sad and devastated their narc friend is, now that you no longer want them. They will be sure to emphasize the brutality in which you used, when throwing a perfectly good relationship with a man that adored you in the trash. What a joke!

Don't let this perfectly executed tactic trip you up. These people were not your friends anyway. Who cares what they think of you. The people that truly know who you are, and what you have been through, will listen, but not believe the made-up rumors.

I'm going to give you some examples of what might take place before, and during the reverse discard. These are some that I have experienced but may not include all that may be used.

- They are irritated by everything you say and do.
- They no longer wish to be around you. They won't even want to look at you.
- They give you the silent treatment.
- They are extra sensitive to everything you say.
- They may have already found new supply and are sneaking around with them while still with you.
- They devalue everything you do to your face, and behind your back.
- They constantly bring up to others, every good deed they have done for you.
- They no longer care about your boundaries. They will purposely say and do things to trigger you in front of others, in order to provoke an argument, or your temper.

When this start happening on a regular basis, be prepared to counteract with the "grey rock" technique. This term describes showing no response at all to their words, or behavior. Don't stoop to their level. You already want out, and now you have your chance. It is so much easier to leave when you know they will gladly let you go. You just have to be prepared to give them what they want and leave. This is their twisted way of opening the door and allowing you to walk away. They are completely done with you.

Amidst all the drama and emotional warfare, you will experience a sense of relief. It is finally over...or is it? Don't be surprised to find them trying to worm their way back into your life a few months, or even years down the road. You know, when that new relationship doesn't work to their advantage, or when they see how successful you have become without them. They will usually wait until they are sure the sting of the final breakup, and all their attempts to tear you down, aren't so fresh in your memory.

Beware! In their mind they have done nothing to persuade you to end it with them. If you reconcile, they will not look like the monster you say they were. You will look indecisive and unstable. Don't discredit yourself and everything they have done to you, by "forgiving and forgetting". The narcissist will never change. Never. I made this mistake two, or three times during my relationship, and it was only a matter of days before the familiar behavior started up again. They want you to look like an indecisive idiot...and you will.

You are better off on your own, then to repeat that chapter again. Learn to love yourself. Learn to trust yourself. There are so many things you could do, besides living for the needs of a selfish parasite. What do you want to do? Where do you want to go? Who do you want to be? These are all your decisions now. The narc is no longer steering **your** ship.

Success and fame are attractions, and attributes that the narcissist wishes to obtain. And, if they are unable to achieve them by their own doing, they will gladly grab on to your success and claim it as their own. They don't want to look like losers in life, so they will search for beautiful and driven partners. They will have nothing but the best in life. As long as it benefits them.

They will still try their damndest to tear you down in private, while "celebrating" your success in public. That is, as long as you are on good terms with them. The minute they see a change of heart; they will no longer cheer you on to others. They will devalue everything you have accomplished, and put a spin on it, to make it look like they were helpful in your triumphs. That is where the "after everything I have done for you" bullshit enters into the picture.

Do not allow yourself to accept what others think of you. Especially those that aren't honest about who they really are. Anyone who spends their life trying to convince others of who they really are, have hidden agendas. The narcissist doesn't even know who they really are. They have been playing their "perfect" part for so long, they have forgotten what it is like to be human. They have no empathy for others. They don't care. They just like to act as if they do when someone is watching.

Actions and words must match, when allowing someone to form an opinion of you. The narcissist is great with words. Just not actions. Nothing will ever match up. They will say one thing and do another. They are the world's worst hypocrites. And when confronted on this, they will have no recollection of saying such a thing. It is comical, when you think about it. How can these people even get away with half the shit they do? Smoke and mirrors. The greatest performers ever to exist. Until you closed the curtain to their stage.

Chapter 10

There Are Good People in the World

After sharing years of my life with a narcissist, I found it hard to believe anyone had any good in them, whatsoever. I looked at the people around me with my built-in filter that I had acquired. You know, the filter that sees past the bullshit someone is trying to sell you. That friendly smile that hides a monster, who only shows up when you get them alone.

I was so afraid to give my attention to anyone. I didn't want to fall into the same trap I spent years planning to escape.

I started to avoid conversation. The less people knew, the better. There for a while, I avoided people and became a recluse. I spent most of my time alone, and learned to love it. There is nothing wrong in doing this. You need to protect what is yours again, and not be so gullible, where matters of the heart are concerned. You had to sift through your dear friends, only to find that most were informants who couldn't wait to share the newfound information that you discreetly shared with them. I found myself wondering if I could ever form a close friendship with anyone ever again?

I saw men as snakes in the grass, lying and waiting vipers ready to attack. I saw the women around me as nothing more than a bunch of gossipy, spill the tea bitches, who you didn't dare trust. I literally had no one I could talk to. I'd go out and have my drinks, while pretending to be in conversation with someone just to pass the time. I never disclosed anything about myself. I was all ears. Silently nodding my head, as if I was really listening to them. My brain was in a fog. A thick fog, made of fake feelings and deceit.

When you find yourself in this situation, and you will, don't panic. You are not ruined. You have just temporarily forgotten that there are still good people in the world. Not everyone is the enemy. Even though it feels that they are. It is normal to form unhealthy opinions about others when you have been severely wounded for so long. You are still in the healing stage, and need to find your peace. I feel that the body allows you to feel this way, because it knows that you need your solitude. You don't want to jump back into anything, just as a temporary band-aid, and regret your decision later. No one is going to help you through this. You know yourself better than anyone else ever will, therefore you need to do this without your quick fix for the night. Don't drag anyone else into your disturbia. Get your shit together first. Then, you can seek out the partner that you deserve. If that is what you choose to do.

I, myself, have chosen to remain single. I don't wish to exert all my energy that I have stored, on chasing the dream of a healthy relationship. I know they exist...I just don't want one right now. I want to put all that energy into myself. I want to invest in my future happiness. Selfish? Absolutely not.

I have been called a man-hater by many for my current status. The status that I have chosen for myself, apparently offends some. Who cares! That is on them. My relationship status in life has nothing to do with them. It is not hurting anyone. It is my choice. I don't HATE anyone. Not even myself, anymore. You don't have to defend your reasons for not wanting to "hook up". When the time is right, you will remember how to ride that bike. Only now, you will have your eyes wide open, and your heart's door safely protected by a security password. It isn't going to open for every friendly smile that comes your way.

I remember the moment, only not the name, of the person that opened my eyes to all of the "good people". It was a welcoming moment that I will never forget. I could have cried right there with relief, but chose to cry later in the privacy of my home. I let all the hate and fear pour out of my eyes and drip to the floor where it belonged. It didn't belong inside of me. I didn't want to hate and think ill of people for the remainder of my life. I wanted the original woman that I once was before the narc. The one who found delight in meeting new people. The one who's heart skipped a beat whenever someone complimented her, or showed her any kindness. But she didn't exist anymore. She had been replaced with a careful woman. A tentative woman.

After living with my head down, afraid to look up, I had forgotten to enjoy the little things that squeeze their way into the mindless routine that I had created for myself to keep busy. The more you fill up your life, the less time you have to think. I didn't want to continue down that dark hole that the narc dug for me. I wanted to stay in the light, so I didn't allow myself to dwell on much. I think I was afraid that I might fall back into "my life wasn't so bad. Maybe I should go back" bullshit. Yes it was bad. That is why you left. Believe it, and move on.

I just got done with my shift, and needed a moment of quiet to decompress from the day, and there he was. A quiet "Hello, how was your day?" seemed innocent enough. And then it happened. Someone was genuinely interested in how my day was. He listened with quiet content.Watching my mouth as I spoke and scanning my face for how I was actually feeling at the moment. He seemed safe. As we spoke, I found myself disclosing things other than just how my day was going.

As I sat there opening up to this absolute stranger, I felt as if I was having an out of body experience. It seemed like someone else was talking. My voice even sounded different. Here was someone who complimented me on my accomplishments, without an agenda. The same accomplishments that I once deemed small and unimportant, because I shared them with the wrong people. They weren't my people. They were the narc's posse. They never truly basked in the light of my delight. They were just collecting information.

But, here was someone who had traveled to the very places you have always dreamed of visiting, with photos and all! Someone, who when they talked, you felt had overcome many challenges, and willingly shared the struggle, along with the outcome. A man that readily, without effort, went out of his way to include his wife in all of these shared moments. He is her friend. A real friend, in every sense of the word. Her confidant. Her partner in life. He purposely made sure that everyone around him was aware of how important she is in his life. All I could do was listen and stare in disbelief. I must have appeared confused. I don't know how I couldn't have, with my mouth agape with surprise, and wide eyes full of awe.

Here was someone that didn't consider the person in their life as a hindrance. As an unwelcome distraction that they were stuck with. Someone who spoke of women as individuals, with interests of their own. As equals, in the realm of humanity. As I sat there mesmerized by it all, I began to feel my frozen heart thaw. The warmth in my chest traveled up my neck and found my hardened mind, which also softened from the unexpected surge of good energy. It filled me with so much warmth, that I felt the tips of my ears and cheeks flush with color. It was like I was brought back to the land of the living. It rekindled the hope that was hiding inside of me. There were good people out there...even men. They are in existence. It reminded me that all men are not just looking for a night of pleasure. All men do not discard your feelings and ignore your dreams. All men are not overgrown, and misbehaving children, who throw raging tantrums when they don't get what they want. All men do not consider their home a prison that they find any excuse to escape, just to get away from you.

It was so endearing to listen to someone who likes to hang out with his wife. Who was there during her time of grief and struggle. Who bragged about her strength and perseverance. Who talked about his job, and interests. Who laughed with you, without judgment. Who seemed to look at you every once in a while, as if to say, "what are you doing here?" Who acted as though I had more opportunities than ever, and was wasting my time stuck here. In the short hour of conversation, I found myself, once again, regretting the time and effort I had spent on all the unfulfilling and uneventful days. All of the nights I spent, just sitting where I was. So much time that was thrown away on all the wrong decisions. The wrong environment. The wrong people that I tried to fit in with, but never were my people. These were not my kindred spirits. All the years I lived, void of encouraging conversation, made me hungry for more. It was like someone flipped the switch to the "on" position. I was finally turned on! And not the way most men think is "turned on". My spark and faith in people had returned.

Thank you universe, or God, or whatever you believe in. Thank you, for reminding me that there are people out there that you had forgotten about, up until now. Now it is up to you to venture out of the comfortable nest that you have placed yourself in, and seek out these people. They are waiting for you. Your true people.

www.ingramcontent.com/pod-product-compliance
Lightning Source LLC
LaVergne TN
LVHW090333210926
848480LV00004B/1401
9798230869306